Where Is
Our Solar System?

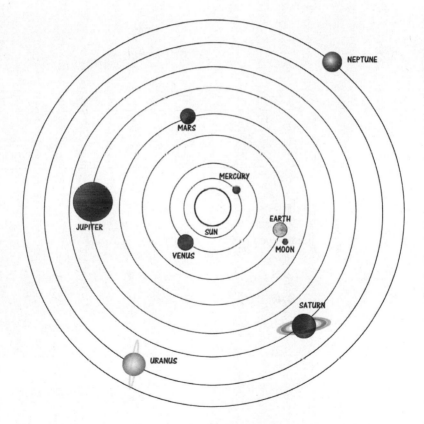

Where Is
Our Solar System?

by Stephanie Sabol

illustrated by Ted Hammond

Penguin Workshop

For Molly and Bennett—SS

To my nephew, Garrett—TH

PENGUIN WORKSHOP
An imprint of Penguin Random House LLC, New York

First published in the United States of America by Penguin Workshop,
an imprint of Penguin Random House LLC, New York, 2018

Visit us online at penguinrandomhouse.com.

Library of Congress Control Number: 2017043834

Printed in the United States of America

ISBN 9780515158182   20 19 18 17

Contents

Where Is Our Solar System?

Thousands of years ago in China, farmers were out in the field working. It had been a sunny day. But suddenly the sky began to darken. This wasn't just a cloud—the sun was disappearing! In a few minutes, the sky was completely dark. The farmers thought they knew what was happening. A dragon was eating the sun.

Quickly, they started to make noise. They chanted songs, beat drums, and banged pots and pans. They had to scare the dragon away. Then the sun would come back. Sure enough, in just a few minutes, it did. Making noise had worked, the farmers believed.

Today we know that a dragon wasn't trying to eat the sun. What those farmers in China saw was a total solar eclipse.

Every year and a half or so, the moon, which is always circling Earth, will get in between the sun and Earth. For a few minutes the moon blocks the sun completely. There is no sunlight.

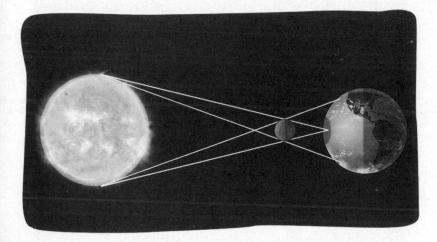

However, in ancient times, the Chinese and other people didn't know the scientific reasons why certain events happened in the natural world. So they made up myths, or stories, to explain them.

The ancient Greeks believed that a group of superhuman gods and goddesses ruled the world. Each morning, one of the gods, Helios, drove a chariot up in the sky, pulling the sun behind him. This was the sunrise. In the evening, he drove back down again. That was the sunset.

Helios pulling the sun across the sky

The Mayans told stories about the moon. There was a moon goddess who fought with the sun, forcing it to go down into the underworld every night. That explained why the sun disappeared whenever the moon came out.

Because of astronomy—the scientific study of objects in space—we know there are no gods or dragons ruling over the heavens. We know that the sun is a star—a star made of hot gas. Eight planets circle, or "orbit," around it, along with comets and asteroids. This is what we call our solar system. And even though we have learned much about it, there are still many things we have yet to discover. The solar system is still a big, exciting mystery.

CHAPTER 1
Sky Watching

Although ancient people didn't understand why many things happened in their world, they were able to learn a lot just by observation. By looking. For instance, from watching the night sky, sailors realized that the position of stars acted like points on a map and helped them navigate their ships.

During the day, the changing position of the sun told the time. Hunters knew to move to new areas when the seasons changed. And farmers saw that certain crops grew better if they were planted during a certain phase of the moon.

The Changing Moon

Sometimes the moon looks like a circle. At other times, it looks like a crescent. Why does the moon change shape? Actually, the moon doesn't change shape. It only appears to. Over the course of a month, the moon reflects a different amount of light from the sun. Sometimes the sun lights up the whole moon. So we see all of it. Other times, it's only partially lit. These changes are known as the phases of the moon.

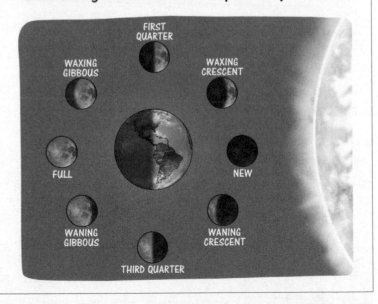

Ancient people also noticed that while some stars seemed to stay fixed in the sky, others moved about. Early Greek stargazers gave these "stars" a special name: *planetes*, which means "wanderer." (It's where we get the word *planet*.) They were able to see five planets with the naked eye—Mercury, Venus, Mars, Jupiter, and Saturn.

Eventually, scientists in ancient Greece became more curious about the science behind the sun, moon, and planets. They wanted to understand *why* the planets moved, and why the moon seemed to change shape.

This led to the beginning of the science of astronomy.

Aristotle was born in Greece about 2,400 years ago. He was a brilliant philosopher and teacher. A philosopher studies different ideas about

Aristotle

the meaning of life and the natural world. Aristotle, who tutored the famous king Alexander the Great, was also an astronomer.

Aristotle realized that the Earth was round. Up until then, people believed the Earth was flat. They thought that if they walked to its edge, they would fall right off. Aristotle proved that the Earth was actually a sphere. How did he know this? He observed that some stars could only be seen from certain places on Earth. If you traveled far away (say from Greece to southern Africa), the stars would no longer be visible. The only explanation

for this was that the Earth was curved and made certain stars disappear from view.

The Greek scientist Ptolemy was born almost five hundred years after Aristotle, around AD 100. He lived

Ptolemy

and worked in Alexandria, Egypt. From watching how the other planets moved, Ptolemy thought that the Earth was the center of the universe. He thought that the other planets and the sun rotated around Earth. He was not correct, but people kept on believing Ptolemy for another 1,400 years!

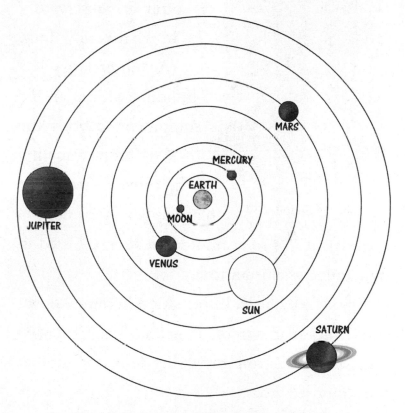

Earth as the center of the universe

During the Middle Ages, astronomy flourished in the Islamic empire that spread over much of the Middle East, North Africa, and Spain. One of the most famous Islamic astronomers was

Omar Khayyam

Omar Khayyam. Khayyam was born in 1048. He built an observatory in what is now Iran. (An observatory is a building with scientific equipment to study the sky.) From watching the movements of the planets, Khayyam made a calendar. It was so accurate that it is still used in Iran and Afghanistan today.

So, little by little, information became known about the solar system. However, truly amazing discoveries in astronomy didn't come for another four hundred years.

CHAPTER 2
A Shocking Idea

In 1473, a man named Nicolaus Copernicus was born in Poland. He was the son of a wealthy businessman. Copernicus grew up to be an astronomer, mathematician, and artist. In 1543, he published a book that shocked everyone. He said that the Earth didn't stay still—it actually followed a path around the sun. So did the other planets. The sun, and not the Earth, was at the center of everything.

Why were so many people outraged by this idea? For so long, what Ptolemy had said was held as true. Most important, the Catholic Church had long accepted the geocentric (Earth-centered) view of the universe. Earth, man's home, must be the most important part of the universe. It *had* to be the center. The Church was very powerful and did not like people speaking against its beliefs. Anyone who did might be jailed or even killed!

Copernicus died the same year his book was published. He didn't have a chance to defend his ideas. However, an Italian astronomer named Galileo Galilei took on that challenge.

Galileo was born in Pisa, Italy, in 1564, the son of an Italian musician. He was an excellent student and liked to test different ideas. (Testing ideas is what all scientists, including astronomers, must do to prove something is true.)

Galileo heard about an invention in the Netherlands called the telescope. It had been

Europe in the 1500s

created by a man named Hans Lippershey, who made eyeglasses. He wanted to make a lens "for seeing things far away as if they were nearby." He put two lenses at either end of a tube, one curved out, one curved in. Looking through it made objects appear much bigger. When Galileo heard about the telescope, he decided to make his own. One that could make objects appear twenty times bigger!

With his telescope, Galileo saw the planet Jupiter had four moons. He also noticed that our moon didn't have a smooth surface—it was covered in mountains, valleys, and craters. Galileo also viewed the different phases of the planet Venus through his telescope. During each phase, Venus would appear to have a different shape because of the reflection of the sun's light on it. To Galileo, this proved that Venus was orbiting the sun and reflecting its light.

Why were these observations so important? They supported Copernicus's belief that the Earth circled the sun and not the other way around.

Galileo was ready to share his beliefs with the world. In 1610, he explained his findings in a book he wrote. It was called *The Starry Messenger*. As Galileo had feared, the Church wanted him to say he was wrong. For years Galileo defended his theories.

Then, in 1633, he was put on trial. The judges were all priests. Galileo was sixty-nine years old. He was tired of defending his ideas. And he was scared of being punished. He knelt before the priests and said he was wrong.

Even so, Galileo was punished. He was put under house arrest. That meant he couldn't leave his home—not ever. So Galileo remained there until his death in 1642. Galileo was right about the solar system but suffered for it. He was a man ahead of his time.

CHAPTER 3
A Tour of the Sun and Stars

By the mid-1700s, the Catholic Church no longer challenged Galileo's ideas. A heliocentric system of the sun with planets orbiting around it became more accepted.

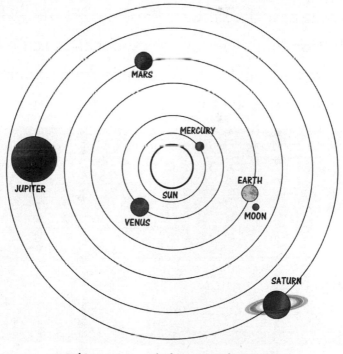

Solar system with the sun at the center

What have we learned about the sun and stars since Galileo's time?

We know that the sun is the *only* star in our solar system. But there are many other solar systems. Scientists have already found five hundred but think there are millions more. These solar systems also have planets and other objects orbiting around them.

The sun is the star closest to Earth. After the sun, the next closest star is Proxima Centauri. The light from our own sun takes about eight minutes to reach us on Earth. The light from Proxima Centauri takes 4.24 years!

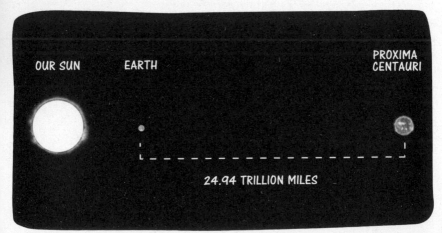

OUR SUN   EARTH   PROXIMA CENTAURI

24.94 TRILLION MILES

Just like other stars, our sun has no solid surface. It is a ball of hot gas—mostly hydrogen and helium. Stars produce heat and light from these gases.

Even though the sun seems gigantic, there are much bigger stars out there. Because they are much farther away, they appear very small to us. We can't see them during the day because our sun is so bright that it blocks their light. At night, those other stars look like tiny pinpricks of light.

All stars are born in giant spinning clouds made of gas and dust. They are called nebulas. Over millions of years, these particles of gas and dust join together and heat up. Once they become hot enough, a star is born.

Stars live very long lives. In fact, even stars that are two hundred million years old are considered young! Young stars are very hot. Their surface temperatures can reach one hundred thousand degrees Fahrenheit. They are usually blue or blue-white in color.

Our sun is a middle-aged star. Even though it is not as hot as a young star, it is still about ten thousand degrees Fahrenheit. Our sun is known as a yellow dwarf star.

All stars eventually run out of fuel. They swell up and get one hundred times bigger. When this happens, they are known as red giant stars. Red giants are huge. Betelgeuse (say: BEE-tull-jooz) is a red supergiant star with a diameter of at least 250 million miles across! If Betelgeuse replaced our sun in the solar system, it would swallow up Mercury, Venus, Earth, and Mars.

After a red giant uses up all its gas fuel, it will shrink down so it's about ten thousand times smaller. Then it is known as a white dwarf. A white dwarf is still very hot. The white dwarf will cool down for billions of years until it dies. Then it is cold, dark, and invisible. It is known as a black dwarf.

One day, our sun will use up its fuel and die. Astronomers don't think that will happen for another five billion years, though.

Supernovas

Different stars lead different kinds of lives. Some stars don't become black dwarfs. Instead, they explode in a flash of light at the end of their lives. These stars are known as supernovas. Supernovas are very rare. In 1054, Chinese astronomers saw a supernova in the sky. Today, people can still see the remains of that explosion with binoculars. It is called the Crab Nebula. It looks like a bright patch of gassy swirls.

CHAPTER 4
The Inner Planets

The ancient Greeks identified five planets with the naked eye: Mercury, Venus, Mars, Jupiter, and Saturn. Later, astronomers discovered two more planets—Uranus and Neptune. Including Earth, there are eight planets. They are divided into two groups: inner planets and outer planets.

The inner planets are the four planets closest to the sun—Mercury, Venus, Earth, and Mars.

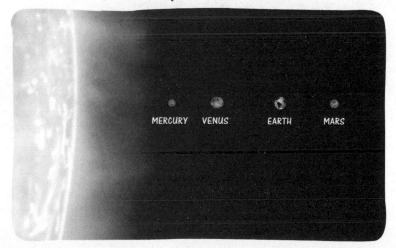

Here's what they have in common: They are small and rocky with solid surfaces. Most of the inner planets are made of heavy metals like iron or nickel. None of them has rings. However, the inner planets are more different from one another than they are alike.

The planet closest to the sun is Mercury. Is it always hot on Mercury? No! The temperature on

Mercury

Mercury goes from very hot during the day to very cold during the night. No other planet has such a dramatic change in temperature.

Mercury is the smallest of the planets. If Earth was the size of a pea, Mercury would be the size of a grain of mustard seed. Even though Mercury is small, it is the fastest planet. Mercury travels up to thirty-one miles per second! It takes Mercury just eighty-eight Earth days to orbit the sun—it travels around the sun four times in one Earth year.

Size comparison between Mercury and Earth

Planets' Names

The planets (except Earth and Uranus) are named after ancient Roman gods.

- Mercury: quick-footed messenger god
- Venus: goddess of love

- Earth: Old English word that means "ground"
- Mars: god of war
- Jupiter: ruler of the gods
- Saturn: father of Jupiter and god of the harvest
- Uranus: Greek god of heaven
- Neptune: god of the sea

Venus

Venus is the second planet from the sun and one of the brightest objects in our sky after the sun and moon. It is known as the Morning Star or Evening Star because it can be seen from Earth shortly before the sun rises and right after the sun sets. It stands out as a tiny white dot near the sun. Sometimes Venus is called Earth's sister planet because they are similar in size.

Size comparison between Venus and Earth

But Venus is very different from Earth. Venus is the hottest planet in our solar system. The temperature on Venus can reach more than 880 degrees Fahrenheit. (So far, the highest temperature ever recorded on Earth has been 134 degrees.)

Until the 1950s, scientists believed Venus was covered with green tropical jungles and swamps. That's not the case. Venus is one of the driest places in the solar system. There is no water at all. Venus is covered with clouds between twenty-eight and forty-three miles thick. These clouds trap heat underneath. It would be impossible for life as we know it to exist on Venus.

The third planet from the sun is our home planet, Earth. Earth is the only planet that isn't named after a god. Earth comes from an Old English word meaning "ground." Earth is very different from the rest of the planets. It contains over eight million different kinds of life. Earth is the only planet in

Mars

our solar system where human beings can live.

The last of the inner planets is Mars. It's about half of Earth's size and covered in rust-colored dust.

Size comparison between Earth and Mars

That's why it's sometimes called the Red Planet.
Mars has two moons—Phobos and Deimos.
These rocky lumps are two of the smallest moons
in the solar system.

Mars has amazing scenery. It is home to
the longest canyon in the solar system, Valles
Marineris. Valles Marineris is four times deeper
and nearly four times longer than the Grand

Canyon. Mars also has a huge volcanic mountain that's sixteen miles high—approximately three times the height of Mount Everest.

Many millions of years ago, Mars may have had oceans and rivers like Earth. So does that mean there was once life on Mars? In order to find out, there have been unmanned space missions to Mars—more than to any other planet. During these missions, spacecraft have flown by, orbited, or landed on Mars so that they can gather information.

One type of spacecraft that has traveled to Mars is a rover. A rover is a robotic vehicle that looks like a big car. It drives over alien terrain while ground

controllers on Earth use computers to direct where it goes. In 2012, a rover named Curiosity landed on Mars. Since then, it has been studying Martian soil, rocks, and dust. So far, no evidence of life on Mars has been found.

Still, people have remained fascinated by the possibility. There are so many books and movies about Martians. Some describe Martians as little green men. In the book *The War of the Worlds,* Martians are violent invaders.

There are also many fan websites. And as Curiosity roams the planet, it tweets information to its millions of followers!

Elon Musk

Scientists aren't the only ones curious about life on Mars. Elon Musk, a wealthy businessman and inventor, says he will find a way to have people live on Mars by the year 2024!

CHAPTER 5
The Outer Planets

In between Mars and Jupiter lies the asteroid belt. (Asteroids are rocky objects that range from twenty feet to hundreds of miles in diameter.) The asteroid belt separates the inner planets from the four outer planets—Jupiter, Saturn, Uranus, and Neptune.

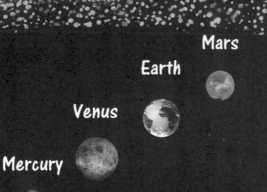

Mars

Earth

Venus

Mercury

Neptune

Uranus

Saturn

Jupiter

Asteroid Belt

Big Crashes

Although most asteroids are found in the asteroid belt, they do exist throughout the solar system. Sixty-five million years ago, a giant asteroid hit the area we now know as Mexico. Many scientists

believe that caused the extinction of dinosaurs. Today, scientists work to detect when asteroids might hit Earth. In 2013, an asteroid entered Earth's atmosphere over a town in Russia. Luckily, the asteroid exploded before it reached the ground.

The outer planets are very different from the inner planets. They are made mostly of gas. And they are big. Really big. The outer planets also have lots of moons. The four outer planets have a total of 146 confirmed moons! (Confirmed means definitely there.) That doesn't even include another twenty-four moons that may exist.

The first of the outer planets is Jupiter. It is about 484 million miles from the sun, and it is the biggest planet in our solar system. If all the other planets were combined into a ball, Jupiter would still be 2.5 times bigger! In 1610, Galileo saw four of Jupiter's moons

Jupiter

with his telescope. So they are called the Galilean moons. But Jupiter has at least sixty-three other moons—more than any other planet.

Size comparison between Earth and Jupiter

There is a Great Red Spot on Jupiter. The Red Spot is so big that two Earths could fit into it.

What is this spot? It is like a hurricane—a storm that has been raging for more than 350 years.

In 1973, a spacecraft named Pioneer 10 flew by Jupiter and sent back the first close-up images of the planet. Several years later, in 1979, the spacecrafts Voyager 1 and Voyager 2 sent back images of Jupiter's moons. Today, Voyager 1 and Voyager 2 are still traveling deeper and deeper into space!

Pioneer 10 exploring space

In 2011, a space probe named Juno launched from Cape Canaveral, Florida. (In Roman mythology, Juno was the wife of Jupiter.) The goal of the Juno mission is to study Jupiter's atmosphere and how Jupiter was made. Juno's trip from Earth to Jupiter took five years! On July 4, 2016, Juno reached Jupiter and began orbiting the planet for twenty months.

Juno with Jupiter

Saturn

Saturn is the second-largest planet in the solar system. It's known for its beautiful rings. All the outer planets have rings. Saturn's, however, are the most visible. These rings are made up of bits of ice, dust, and rocks. No one knows for sure where Saturn's rings came from. Some scientists think they were made from leftover materials after Saturn first formed. Others think they might be bits of moons and asteroids.

Size comparison between Earth and Saturn

Galileo first spotted Saturn's rings in his telescope, but he didn't know what they were. He thought he was looking at a planet with handles. Saturn's rings are massive—three miles thick. Yet if Saturn were the size of a basketball, its rings would be thinner than a single strand of hair.

Both Jupiter and Saturn are made up of hydrogen and helium. Sometimes they are called the gas giants. It would be impossible to stand on these planets, since they are made of gas. However, it's likely they have a small center made of liquid or rock.

The next planet, Uranus, is also made of hydrogen and helium. Uranus also contains methane gas, which gives it a blue color. The most

Uranus

unusual feature of Uranus is that it spins on its side! Astronomers think it was hit by something huge long ago, which knocked it off a vertical spin.

Size comparison between
Earth and Uranus

Uranus was discovered in Great Britain in 1781 by William Herschel. It was the first planet that was discovered by using a telescope. Telescopes had become more powerful since Galileo's time. Herschel thought he was looking at a comet. But he came to realize it was a planet.

Uranus is known as an icy giant, not a gas giant. It is very cold. But it's not as cold as the planet farthest from the sun—Neptune.

Another icy giant, Neptune was first identified as a planet in 1846. Neptune's weather is very wild. Winds can reach speeds of over 1,500 miles per hour. (A Category 5 hurricane on Earth has winds of 157 miles per hour or more.) As the

Neptune

most distant planet from the sun, Neptune has a very long orbit. It takes Neptune 165 Earth years to complete a trip around the sun!

Size comparison between Earth and Neptune

The solar system doesn't end after Neptune. Outside of Neptune's orbit lies the Kuiper Belt (say: KY-purr). It contains bits of rock and ice, comets, and dwarf planets. The most famous dwarf planet is Pluto. Pluto was once counted as

the ninth planet in our solar system. But in 2006, it was downgraded.

Scientists have long debated what makes a planet. In 2006, they came up with an answer. They said a planet must do three things. First, it must orbit the sun. Second, a planet has to be shaped like a sphere. And lastly, a planet must not have any debris or other objects (not counting moons) in its way as it orbits the sun. A planet has to have enough of a gravitational field to force those smaller objects out of its path.

Pluto is round and orbits the sun. But objects like ice do get in the way of Pluto as it travels around the sun. (It's not strong enough for them to move out of its way.) So far, that is why Pluto is no longer considered a planet.

However, some scientists disagree with this definition. Perhaps one day there will be new rules for what makes a planet. Maybe Pluto will be let back in.

Comets

One of the most brilliant objects in the night sky is a comet. Comets are frozen balls of ice a few miles wide. The word *comet* comes from the Greek word *kometes*, which means "long haired." That's because as a comet travels, it begins to defrost and may form a beautiful long tail, sometimes millions of miles long. Comets come from two places—the Kuiper Belt or the Oort Cloud. The Oort Cloud is even farther out in space.

CHAPTER 6
Return to Earth

In 1994, an American astronomer named Carl Sagan published a book called *Pale Blue Dot*. What was the dot?

Earth!

That's what Earth looks like from space. Just a tiny blue dot. Sagan wrote, "Look . . . at that dot. That's here. That's home. That's us. On it everyone you love, everyone

Carl Sagan

you know, everyone you ever heard of, every human being who ever was, lived out their lives."

Earth is a special place. Not only is Earth inhabited by animals (including humans!), it also has plants and fungi. Why is there all this life?

One of the reasons is the location of our planet. Earth is the perfect distance from the sun. If it were closer, everything would burn up. If it were farther away, everything would freeze and die.

Another reason Earth has so much life is because of water. Earth is the only planet to have water in all three states: solid (ice), liquid (rain), and gas (steam). More than 70 percent of the Earth is covered with liquid water. Water is essential for life. Scientists believe the first forms of life on Earth started in our oceans.

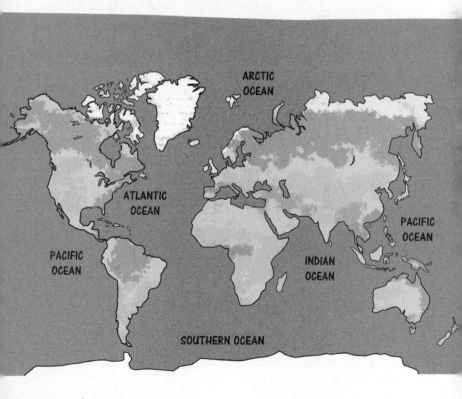

Earth is about ninety-three million miles from the sun. That's hard to imagine. So think of it this way: You are on a basketball court. You place the basketball on the ground at one end of the court. The basketball is the sun. Then you walk across the entire court, ninety-four feet. At the other end, you place a very tiny head of a pin on the ground. That is the Earth. Wow! How tiny the Earth is and how far away from the sun.

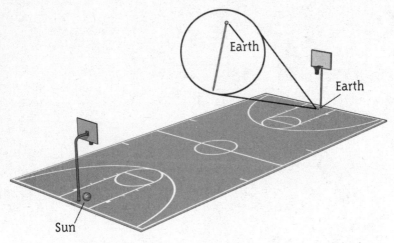

Earth

Earth

Sun

Now imagine the pinhead has an invisible line going through its center from top to bottom. That's called an axis. The axis is tilted so Earth

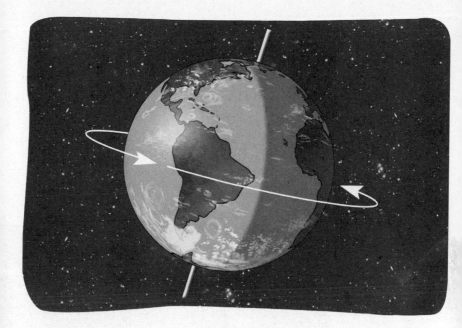

tips a little on its side. Earth is always spinning on its axis. It takes twenty-four hours, one day, for a complete spin. For half that time, part of the Earth faces the sun and is in daylight. The other side of the Earth faces away from the sun. It is night there. When it's the middle of the day in New York, it's the middle of the night in China. But, as the Earth continues turning, eventually it will become night in New York and day in China.

Earth travels all the way around the sun every 365.25 days—one year. Imagine the basketball court again. The basketball stays where it is, but the pinhead starts moving. It travels in an oval path and stays between ninety-one and ninety-four feet from the basketball. Sometimes it moves a little closer to or farther from the

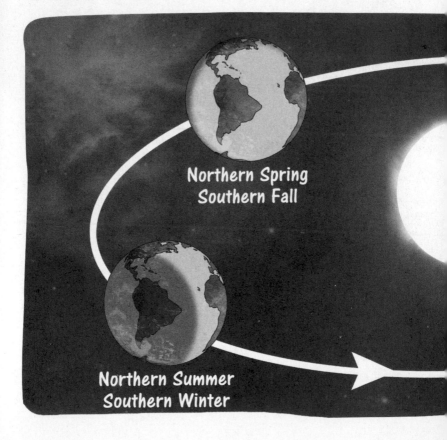

Northern Spring
Southern Fall

Northern Summer
Southern Winter

basketball. That's Earth's orbit.

Since Earth's axis is slightly tilted, for part of the year the northern half of the planet is pointed toward the sun. It gets more direct sunlight then, so that area of the Earth has summer. During that same time, the southern half is tilted away from the sun. It has winter.

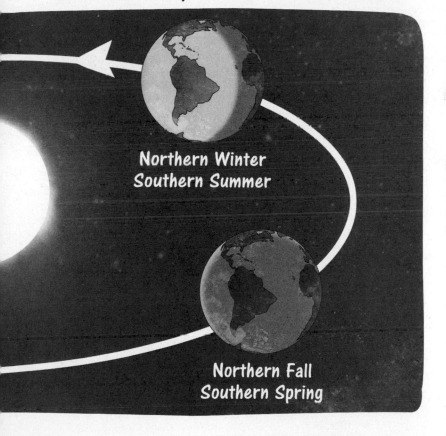

Northern Winter
Southern Summer

Northern Fall
Southern Spring

Earth formed about 4.6 billion years ago, at the same time as the rest of our solar system. Earth was just a young planet when a big object slammed into it. This is what caused the Earth to tilt on its axis. Big pieces of the Earth were blown out! Those pieces of Earth became our moon. The moon is our closest neighbor in space, and orbits around Earth as Earth travels around the sun.

What would happen if there were no moon? Nights would be very dark (no moonlight!) and the ocean tides would be much lower. That's because the moon's gravity pulls on Earth's oceans and makes the tides rise and fall. Gravity is the pulling force that holds things together and stops them from floating away into space. The pull of the moon's gravity also makes Earth rotate more slowly. Without the moon, a day on Earth would be much shorter—between six to twelve hours shorter. Most importantly, the moon helps to control our weather. Because of the moon's gravity, Earth's axis stays tilted. This helps control Earth's seasons. Without the tilt of the axis, Earth might have very extreme seasons or no seasons at all. Many living beings wouldn't be able to survive in this kind of climate.

Earth is the only place in the solar system where we are sure life exists. But our solar system is only a very small part of the entire universe. What else is out there?

CHAPTER 7
Beyond Our Solar System

On a clear night, you can see thousands of stars in the sky. But they are not part of our solar system. Our solar system only has one star, the sun.

So where *are* all of these other stars?

The stars are in our galaxy. A galaxy is a giant group of stars, gas, and dust. Each galaxy is like a city of stars. Our galaxy is called the Milky Way. It is huge. It contains our sun and more than two hundred billion other stars.

The Milky Way's shape is a spiral. From above, the Milky Way looks like a pinwheel with long, spiraling arms. Some galaxies are shaped like an oval. And some galaxies have no special shape— they just look like big blobs!

Our Solar System

Milky Way

Our solar system is located in one of the smaller arms of the Milky Way, called the Orion Arm. The Orion Arm is named after the constellation Orion. Orion was a hunter in Greek mythology.

Constellations

A constellation is a group of stars. Long ago, people would imagine drawing lines from star to star to make pictures, usually of animals or mythic heroes. A total of eighty-eight constellations light up the night sky. The constellations you see depend on where you are on Earth. Some are only visible from the Northern Hemisphere and some only from the Southern Hemisphere.

Here are some of the most famous constellations:

Ursa Major means "Great Bear" in Latin. Seven stars within Ursa Major are known as the "Big

Dipper" in North America. A dipper is like a ladle for serving soup.

Big Dipper

Ursa Minor (Little Bear) contains Polaris, the North Star. Polaris is located almost directly above the North Pole.

Canis Major means "Great Dog" in Latin. It contains Sirius, the brightest star in the night sky, known as the "Dog Star."

Hydra is the largest constellation. Hydra means "Water Snake" in Latin. And it does indeed slither across the sky.

In Greek myths, Orion was known as a great hunter with a shield and an unbreakable club.

Orion

The name of our galaxy came from the ancient Romans. They noticed that a band of stars in the night sky looked like milk. They named it *via lactea*, Milky Way. Other cultures have different names for our galaxy. People from Scandinavia call it "Winter Street" because the galaxy is more visible during the winter. The Japanese call it the "River of Heaven." The Cherokee name for the Milky Way means "the place where the dog ran." They tell a folktale of a dog that stole some cornmeal and was chased away. The cornmeal spilled across the sky and created the galaxy.

Up until the early 1900s, astronomers believed that the Milky Way was the entire universe. Nothing more existed. That changed in the 1920s, when an American astronomer named Edwin Hubble looked through a very powerful telescope at an observatory in California. This telescope was one hundred inches wide—much bigger than handheld telescopes were.

Hubble studied a distant star through the telescope. He made some measurements and realized that the star was so far away that it could not be part of the Milky Way. It had to be in another galaxy. Hubble's calculations showed that the Milky Way was just one of many galaxies in a huge universe. The universe was much larger and more complicated than anyone thought.

Scientists now believe there are one hundred billion galaxies in the universe. We can see three of those galaxies with the naked eye: the Andromeda Galaxy, and the Large and Small Magellanic Clouds.

Andromeda Galaxy

Andromeda was named after a beautiful princess from Greek mythology. The Large and Small Magellanic Clouds were named after the sixteenth-century Portuguese explorer Ferdinand Magellan.

Magellanic Clouds

He led the first expedition that sailed around the entire Earth.

All galaxies keep stretching, or expanding. Imagine blowing a bubble with bubble gum. In the beginning, the gum is small and thick. But as you keep blowing, the bubble stretches wider and wider. That's what is happening with the galaxies.

So just where did our universe come from? Astronomers have a theory called the Big Bang.

A theory is an explanation for how things happen. Theories are based on ideas that scientists test over and over.

The Big Bang theory says that about 13.8 billion years ago, all the stars, galaxies, and planets looked nothing like they do now. They were just tiny particles mixed with light and energy. No one really knows where any of it came from.

Astronomers believe these particles all joined together at a single tiny point. This tiny point was very dense and extremely hot and created atoms. (Atoms are the basic building blocks for everything in the universe.) The atoms then grouped together to form stars. Over time, the first stars and galaxies came into being. Later came planets and asteroids. The Big Bang was the moment the universe began to expand. It was the beginning of space and time.

Timeline of Life on Earth

13.8 billion years ago: Big Bang—the universe begins

13.4 billion years ago: The first stars and galaxies appear

11 billion years ago: The Milky Way begins to form

4.6 billion years ago: The sun and planets begin to form

3.8 billion years ago: The first life appears on Earth

200,000 years ago: Modern humans first appear

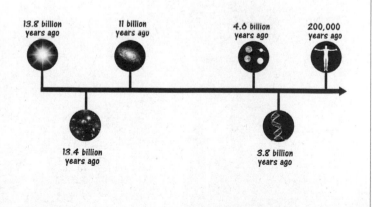

CHAPTER 8
The Space Race

In 1961, President John Fitzgerald Kennedy (JFK) made an important speech before a large audience in Houston, Texas. He declared that the United States would land a man on the moon! And it would happen before 1970.

JFK convinced the US Congress to pour millions

of dollars into the US space program. It was called NASA (National Aeronautics and Space Administration).

Why did JFK want the United States to get to the moon so quickly? One reason was to show up the Soviet Union. The Soviet Union had fought on the same side as the United States during World War II. However, after the war ended, the Soviet Union and the United States became enemies. The US government didn't want the Soviet Union to get too powerful and try to rule other countries. One way to show power was to succeed in space missions.

Space begins about sixty miles above Earth. The Soviet Union had launched a space program in 1957. The first man-made satellite was sent into space. A satellite is an object placed in orbit to gather information. The Soviet satellite was called Sputnik 1 and was able to orbit the Earth in just one hundred minutes!

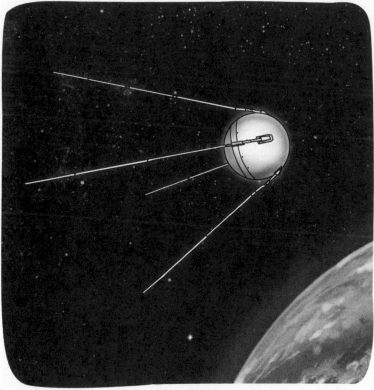

Sputnik 1

The US government was worried. What if the Soviets made weapons factories in space and dropped missiles down on other countries? The United States wanted to get satellites in space, too. The Soviet Union had talked about landing a man on the moon. So the United States wanted to do it first.

The space race was on!

Over the next few years, the Soviets had more success with space exploration than the United States did. In 1961, Russian Yuri Gagarin

Yuri Gagarin

became the first man in space. The Soviets called their space travelers *cosmonauts*. (*Cosmonaut* means "sailor of the universe.") Americans used the term *astronaut*, which means "sailor of the stars."

In 1961, NASA began the Apollo program. The goal of the Apollo program was to send astronauts to the moon and bring them back. Each Apollo mission was numbered.

Tragically, Apollo 1 ended even before it launched. Three astronauts were killed on the ground by a fire inside the test command center.

In December of 1968, Apollo 8 launched. It became the first spacecraft to orbit the moon. On Christmas Eve, the astronauts appeared on a televised broadcast. They beamed back pictures they had taken of the Earth and moon, and read from the Bible.

Launch of Apollo 8

Even by the start of the last year of the decade—1969—the United States still had not reached the moon. But neither had the Russians. On July 16, Apollo 11 launched. Buzz Aldrin, Neil Armstrong, and Michael Collins were the three American astronauts on board. It took three

The *Eagle* landing on the moon

days to travel from Earth to the moon. Once they arrived, Collins stayed in the spacecraft while Armstrong and Aldrin transferred to a smaller craft named the *Eagle*. As soon as it touched down on the moon's surface, Armstrong reported, "The *Eagle* has landed."

Armstrong stepped outside of the craft and placed his foot on the moon. He said, "That's one small step for [a] man, one giant leap for mankind." Together, Armstrong and Aldrin walked on the moon for over two hours, collecting samples and taking photographs. They also left an American flag on a flagpole. Millions of people all over the world watched the two astronauts on their televisions. When the astronauts returned home, they were welcomed as heroes. JFK was no longer alive, but his dream had come true.

Neil Armstrong

After the moon landing of 1969, there were several more Apollo missions. In 1972, the crew of Apollo 17 sent a photograph of Earth from space. The photo shows what became known as the Blue Marble, because that's what Earth looked like!

Apollo 17 was the last Apollo mission. By 1972, a total of twelve astronauts had walked on the moon. Once the United States had completed these missions first, the Soviet Union wasn't interested in going to the moon anymore.

The space race ended in 1975. Exploration of space, however, still goes on. Many different missions have gone to space since the space race ended.

CHAPTER 9
Life in Space

In 1984, President Ronald Reagan announced that the United States was going to build the first permanent space station. A space station is a large spacecraft where astronauts live for an extended period of time. President Reagan said, "We can . . . [continue] working in space for peaceful, economic, and scientific gain."

Reagan asked other countries to join the United States in building the station. Space programs from Russia, Japan, Canada, and the European Space Agency joined with the United States to build the International Space Station (ISS).

The ISS was so big that it had to be sent to space in parts. The first part was launched in 1998. From the front, the ISS resembles a giant butterfly. A center part connects side panels called solar arrays. They look like wings. The solar arrays capture energy from the sun. The energy is then converted to electricity.

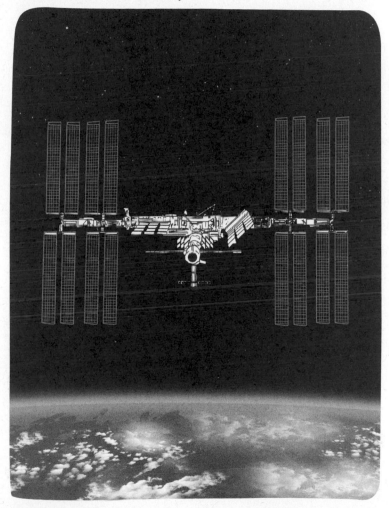

The ISS is the largest man-made object in space—as big as a football field! It orbits the Earth from more than two hundred miles away. Still, at night it's possible to see the ISS from Earth.

Six astronauts can live in the ISS at one time. The station has five bedrooms, two bathrooms, and even a gym. There is a big window from which to view Earth. The ISS takes about ninety minutes to orbit the Earth. So every day, the astronauts see sixteen sunrises and sixteen sunsets from that window!

The ISS is a giant floating space lab. Astronauts spend months studying how humans and other animals react to life in space. They also grow plants and gather information that may be useful someday if people are living in space colonies. Some ISS studies have even helped humans on Earth. They found that a breathing device used on the space station can help people who suffer from asthma to breathe easier.

Astronauts do the same things we do on Earth. They eat, sleep, and use the bathroom. But doing those things is very different in space. There is no gravity. Astronauts must use seatbelts when they use the toilet. Otherwise they would float away! They sleep in bags strapped down with Velcro.

Eating and drinking in space can be tricky, too. You can only drink liquid from a straw. Otherwise the liquid would float like a blob in the air. Imagine a squiggly blob of orange juice floating past you! Food isn't very tasty, either. It comes in small packets and is dehydrated. That means all the water is taken out of it. Many astronauts add spices to their food to make it taste better. Spicy food also helps keep the astronauts' noses from getting too stuffy—something that happens often in space.

It's hard work to be an astronaut, and it can be lonely. American astronaut Scott Kelly spent nearly a year aboard the ISS from 2015 to 2016. It was difficult to be away from his family for so long. But it was important work. He said, "I believe in the importance of flying in space and the research that we do."

CHAPTER 10
Life Beyond Our Solar System?

For thousands of years, people have wondered if life exists anywhere else in our solar system. We know our planet is rich with life. Scientists estimate that there are more than 7.5 million species yet to be discovered on Earth! This number includes fish, fungi, insects, and land animals—and *doesn't* include bacteria. There is so much life on Earth that it's hard to believe that none has been found yet anywhere else.

Where else in our solar system *could* life exist?

Scientists think it's possible on two of Jupiter's moons and on two of Saturn's. Jupiter's moon Europa is the most likely place to have life. Europa has a thick icy crust—as hard as granite. But under that icy crust lies a liquid ocean with more water

Europa

Jupiter

than Earth has. The ocean gets no sunlight, which would make it difficult for even microscopic life to exist. However, some sea life on Earth has survived in very harsh environments like this.

Titan, one of Saturn's moons, is the second-largest moon in the solar system. Titan's atmosphere has methane. Scientists are puzzled about why methane exists on Titan. Earth has methane because living organisms create it. Does that mean that Titan has similar organisms living far below the surface? Maybe. But it's very cold on Titan. Perhaps too cold for life. One of Saturn's other moons has qualities that might make it possible for life to exist—but nothing is confirmed.

Will we find aliens or intelligent life in our solar system? Scientists definitely don't think so. But there are hundreds of planets circling nearby stars. Is there intelligent life on one of them? Scientists want to find out. In 2009, NASA launched the

Kepler mission. It was named after the German astronomer Johannes Kepler, who lived from 1571 to 1630. Kepler is who explained that all the planets move around the sun in an elliptical (oval) path.

Johannes Kepler

The Kepler spacecraft is looking for Earth-like planets in other solar systems. Maybe those planets will have life like ours on them. So far the Kepler spacecraft has discovered nine planets that are the same size as Earth and are the same distance from their sun. Over time, astronomers will find out what does—or does not—exist on them.

SETI

SETI stands for the Search for Extraterrestrial Intelligence. The SETI project started in 1959 to look for intelligent life in space. Since then, radio messages have been sent into the universe in hopes that an alien civilization will receive them and respond. Radio messages are used because they can travel very far distances and still keep their power. So far, no messages have been sent back.

Unidentified Flying Objects (UFOs)

The term *UFO* was first used in the 1950s by the United States Air Force to describe any flying object that couldn't be identified. Today, most people think of alien spaceships when they hear the phrase. Hundreds of UFO sightings are reported every year.

The most famous UFO incident occurred in 1947 in Roswell, New Mexico. A large object crashed into a ranch. Some people suspected aliens were inside. But the US Air Force said it was a weather balloon.

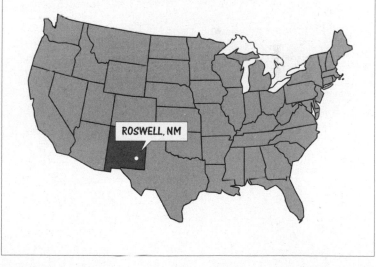

ROSWELL, NM

Why are humans so interested in finding out whether there's life in places other than Earth? Well, it's fascinating to consider that we may not be alone in the vast universe. Maybe there are beings in another solar system that can help us solve some of the problems we face on Earth.

CHAPTER 11
The Future

In 1998, an American astrophysicist named Neil deGrasse Tyson wrote, "We are not simply in the universe; we are part of it. We are born from it. One might even say we have been empowered by the universe to figure itself out—and we have only just begun."

The universe is nearly fourteen billion years old, but astronomers have only really started to understand it in the past one thousand years. There are still many questions. However, even without all the answers, there are theories about what will happen to our sun, Earth, galaxy, and universe.

Without the sun, there can be no life on Earth. What will happen when the sun becomes a red giant in five billion years? Mercury and Venus will burn up right away. It's likely that Earth will, too. But even if Earth doesn't burn up, it will still be so hot that life will no longer be able to survive. Land animals will be the first to go. The Earth's surface will be too hot for them. Humans could build shelters underground, where it will be cooler. However, soon the oceans will dry up and sea life will die. Our atmosphere will grow hotter, and plants will die. Once the plants are gone, there won't be enough oxygen in the environment for humans to breathe. Humans will die, too.

The death of the sun isn't the only dramatic event that will happen in our universe. The Milky Way will someday smash into the neighboring galaxy, Andromeda. Together they will form an elliptical-shaped galaxy that astronomers have nicknamed "Milkomeda." That's a combination of the names of the two galaxies. This won't happen for billions of years, though. But even if it were to happen next year, we might not even notice. Galaxies are so spread out that our solar system probably wouldn't feel the impact of such a crash.

This is how "Milkomeda" might look.

We know what will happen to our sun and the Earth. We even know what will happen to our galaxy. But what will happen to our entire universe? The truth is, nobody knows for certain.

One theory is called the Big Chill. During the Big Chill, the universe will slowly drift apart. No new stars will be born, and already-existing ones will burn out and die. Trillions of years from now, there will be nothing left.

In the Big Rip theory, the universe will expand faster and faster. Planets, galaxies, and stars will explode!

Another theory is the Big Crunch. The Big Crunch is the opposite of the Big Bang. The universe will stop expanding and start crunching together instead. Everything will come together into a single point before it disappears forever.

Billions of years is a very long time. Nobody alive on Earth today has to worry about the sun burning up or the Milky Way crashing into Andromeda.

Instead, scientists and astronomers will continue to learn more. They will send missions farther and farther into space. Maybe they will even find life on a faraway planet.

The rest of us on Earth will learn along with them. In the meantime, we will gaze up into the heavens and realize how remarkable it is to be alive on planet Earth—our very special pale blue dot.

A New Solar System

In February 2017, NASA made an exciting announcement. Seven planets were found orbiting a red dwarf star called TRAPPIST-1. The rocky planets orbiting the star are all about the same size as Earth—and a few might be able to support life!

If our sun were as big as a basketball, TRAPPIST-1 would be as small as a golf ball. It is much cooler, too. TRAPPIST-1 is about 4,150 degrees Fahrenheit— less than half the temperature of our sun. The planets are much closer to it. That means that some of the planets might be at the right temperature to have water, or even oceans, on them—a promising sign for life.

TRAPPIST-1 can be found in the constellation Aquarius. It is a whopping 235 trillion miles away from Earth—but it's still one of the three hundred closest stars to our sun.

Scientists will search for evidence of life on TRAPPIST-1's planets. Thomas Zurbuchen from NASA said, "Are we alone out there? We're making a step forward with this—a leap forward, in fact—towards answering that question."

Timeline of Our Solar System

bya = billion years ago

c. 4.6 bya	The sun and planets begin to form
350 BC	Aristotle states that the Earth is a sphere
AD 1543	Copernicus shares his belief in a sun-centered solar system
1610	Galileo sees four moons orbiting Jupiter
1781	William Herschel discovers Uranus
1846	Neptune is discovered
1961	Cosmonaut Yuri Gagarin is the first human to go into space
1969	Neil Armstrong is the first man to walk on the moon
1972	Apollo 17 takes a photo of Earth from space, known as the Blue Marble
1977	Voyager 2 and Voyager 1 launch
1994	Carl Sagan publishes *Pale Blue Dot*
1998	The first piece of the International Space Station launches into orbit
2006	Pluto is demoted to dwarf planet
2012	The rover Curiosity lands on Mars

Timeline of the Earth

mya = million years ago

c. 4.6 bya	Earth begins as a small rocky object
c. 3.8 bya	The first life appears on Earth
c. 65 mya	Dinosaurs die out, possibly because of an asteroid that struck Earth
c. 7-6 mya	The first early humans appear on Earth
200,000 years ago	The first "modern" humans appear in Africa
c. AD 100	Ptolemy is born in ancient Egypt
1054	Chinese astronomers observe the Crab Nebula supernova
1929	Edwin Hubble publishes his findings that there are more galaxies than just the Milky Way
1947	An unidentified flying object crashes in Roswell, New Mexico
1958	National Aeronautics and Space Administration (NASA) is formed
1959	The Search for Extraterrestrial Intelligence (SETI) project begins
1961	JFK declares that the United States will put a man on the moon by the end of the decade
1975	The Apollo program ends
1980	Ronald Reagan is elected president of the United States
1991	The Soviet Union collapses
2009	NASA spacecraft telescope Kepler launches

Bibliography

*Books for young readers

*Aguilar, David A. *Space Encyclopedia: A Tour of Our Solar System and Beyond.* Washington, DC: National Geographic Kids, 2013.

Chown, Marcus. *Solar System: A Visual Exploration of the Planets, Moons, and Other Heavenly Bodies That Orbit Our Sun.* New York: Black Dog & Leventhal, 2011.

Dinwiddie, Robert, Heather Couper, John Farndon, Nigel Henbest, David Hughes, Giles Sparrow, Carole Stott, and Colin Stuart. *The Planets: The Definitive Visual Guide to Our Solar System.* New York: DK, 2014.

Petersen, Carolyn Collins. *Astronomy 101: From the Sun and Moon to Wormholes and Warp Drive, Key Theories, Discoveries, and Facts about the Universe.* Avon, MA: F&W Media, 2013.

*Simon, Seymour. *Our Solar System.* New York: HarperCollins, 2014.

*Simon, Seymour. *Stars.* New York: HarperCollins, 2006.

*Stott, Carole. *I Wonder Why Stars Twinkle and Other Questions about Space.* New York: Kingfisher, 2011.

Website

www.nasa.gov